Sorter Field Manual

Sorting Grading Classing

Creating Standardization Across the USA

Fiber Sorter Training

www.sortgradeclass.com
info@fibersorting.com

Table of Contents

How To Documents 44

SORTING, GRADING, CLASSING (SGC)

JOB DESCRIPTION

FIBER SORTER & GRADER

Sorters trained in this program, apprentice and in receipt of their Master Certificate, are required to accomplish the following:

Pre-education of their clients – Send to your clients prior to sorting appointment the pre education documents required. Make sure you fully understand what your client wants to accomplish with their fiber. It is especially important that you determine where your client is going to send their fiber for processing and if it will or will not be dehaired since this directly impacts your sorting.

Sort the fiber in an **accurate** and **efficient** manner – Maintain procedures (the sorter checklist will help you) and paperwork; sort fiber in a reasonable time frame.

Post- Sorting Education – Based on the results of the fiber sorting, reconcile the initial fiber goals with what the producer's fiber can actually achieve, complete and explain the inventory sheet.

Follow up – Make sure there are no additional questions from your client. Ensure your client fully understands how to read the sort records and the inventory sheet.

Data Base Entry on every client as required – accurately recording all bags of fiber sorted except for Mixed Grade.

INSTRUCTOR BIOGRAPHIES

Wini Labrecque

Wini Labrecque
Star Weaver Farm/SWF Fiber
Innovations
swffiber@zoominternet.net
724-272-4285

Wini Labrecque has been involved in the fiber industry since the late 1980s. With a focus on natural fibers, she has developed an extensive background in utilization and promotion of all types of fibers for practical and commercial use. Wini is a weaver, hand spinner, felter, knitter, crocheter and dyer.

She is an AOA Certified Alpaca Fleece judge, Certified Camelid Fiber Grader/Sorter/Classer through Olds College in Canada, Trained Grader/Sorter of cashmere fiber as well as trained in judging cashmere. Wini is working with a company to help develop better cashmere production, collection and marketing with nomad people of Kyrgyzstan. Working with IYAK (Int'l Yak Association) she has been instrumental in developing criteria and judging protocol for yak fiber both on and off the animal. Wini is a past founding partner in a company dedicated to utilization of all grades of alpaca fiber into woven fabric for home décor use.

A retired Veterinary Assistant, Wini and her husband John have raised alpacas, cashmere producing goats, angora goats, sheep and angora rabbits over the years. They currently have 5 alpacas including 1 suri that are utilized for fiber production. Wini's background gives her the unique opportunity to share her knowledge with others to help enhance their own livestock programs.

Jody Hezoucky

Jody Hezoucky
Lana Bella Alpaca Farm
info@4alpaca.com or barngodess12@gmail.com
330-627-6000 cell 330-289-7138
www.4alpaca.com

Jody and her family started raising alpacas in Hudson Ohio 1997. In 2004 they moved to a 53 acre farm in Carrollton, Ohio. Lana Bella Alpaca Farm is home to over 25 alpacas, 3 dogs, and 2 cats.

Jody's husband Frank is a project manager at Hendrickson during the week, but has managed to transform Lana Bella Alpaca Farm into a showplace for visitors. She has 2 sons Derek and Deven.

Jody graduated from Kent State University with a BA in Marketing and a BA in Transportation and Logistics. She worked as a transportation specialist for over 15 years before being able to stay home with the boys and the alpacas.

In 2008 Jody was researching possible outlets for their fiber and was recommended by a client to research Coarse Broads and the NFP fiber cooperative. That led to inviting Coarse Broads to their farm to give the Fiber sorting for maximum profit seminar to more than 20 local breeders.

That was the eye opening experience she needed. Jody traveled to Harrisville, NH in spring of 09 for the sorting certification class and was certified by Aug. 09.

Jody current manages the product distribution for NFP members and enjoys applying her transportation knowledge to help keep freight cost to a minimum. She joined the Certified Sorted System team as a Teacher/Mentor and looks forward to educating and helping all breeders interested in getting their fleeces to market.

Pam Ellenberger

Pam Ellenberger
Bent Limb Farm
Cell 484 797 2263
pellenbergerrcf8@gmail.com

Pam Ellenberger & her husband, Paul Stelmach, live in Shoemakersville, PA (northeast of Reading, PA) on 55 acres. They bought their first alpaca in February 2009 and Pam discovered sorting the same year. She took the course in October 2009 and became a Certified Sorter in the fall of 2011. She began teaching sorting to others soon after her certification and joined Certified Sorted Systems as a partner to increase the number of sorters available across the country.

Pam has been knitting for over 40 years and came to alpacas because of their luxurious fiber. Since owning alpacas, she has expanded into spinning, weaving and felting. Playing with color via dyeing and blending expands her creativity with beautiful results. Angora rabbits—Satin, French & Giant—add to the fiber mix on the farm.

The need for quality control, standardization and a North American commercial alpaca fiber industry seemed obvious to her if the alpaca breeders were to not only survive, but thrive. Pam's goal for sorting was to be able to help other alpaca owners generate income for their farm by getting the fleece into production. Her focus on productivity is a bonus for her clients since she remains current with the possible options available in the marketplace for natural fiber production.

Brian Willsey

Brian Willsey
314.681.9211
brian.willsey@hotmail.com
www.rwalpaca.com

Brian, his wife Theresa and his parents live on a 64 acre ranch in Owensville, MO – Missouri wine country. They raise alpacas (both huacaya and suri) and Tunis sheep The alpacas and sheep are raised for wool. They also produce grass-fed lamb.

Brian became interested in the NFP cooperative when he attended a seminar by Coarse Broads funded by MOPACA, the Midwest Alpaca Owners and Breeders Association. After becoming a member of the co-op, he decided to become a Certified Sorter, took the class in 2008 and was certified in 2011.

Alpaca fiber and sheep wool are both sorted and sent to the cooperative. Coarser fleece is processed personally and value-added through a 66" Feltloom. Any fine but inconsistent fiber is processed into a farm yarn for value adding and retail through the retail outlet onsite.

His background is in commercial reproduction, and has over 25 years in the printing industry. One of his primary responsibilities has been training. With SGC, he will have the opportunity to help train other sorters.

Chapter 1:
BEING A SORTER

SORTER RESPONSIBILITIES APPRENTICE / **MASTER:**

✔ BE PROFESSIONAL

✔ BE EFFICIENT AND TIMELY

✔ BE ACCURATE

✔ BE COMPLETE - FINISH THE JOB

BE PROFESSIONAL

This is your business and you work as an independent contractor. As with any professional training organization, to remain affiliated with Sorting Grading Classing (SGC) requires that certain standards be met. Professional conduct is of the highest importance. Conducting your business in a professional manner not only enhances and grows your business, but also enhances the sorting community as a whole.

Professional conduct includes being positive and constructive with your clients and other sorters. What you say and do reflects on sorters in general, especially SGC with which you are affiliated.   Although sorting is often done in jeans and a t-shirt, you should be no less professional than someone who reports to the office in a suit. Conduct yourself as a professional, acting and speaking in a manner that will add to your credibility and that of your fellow sorters. Honesty, hard-work and ethical conduct is imperative.

Confidentiality is important to protect yourself and the clients you sort for. The information you glean from sorting someones fiber is confidential - what you learn there on that farm stays on the farm! This is one of the reasons that Individual Sort Records are not routinely kept by the sorter and become the confidential property of the fiber producer. Copies of Inventory Sheets are essential for the sorter to complete their work, but copies of Individual Sort Records should be limited to the times that you bag sort and send the results via email to the fiber producer. In that instance it is important to keep an electronic copy until the producer assures you that they have received the Individual Sort Records for each animal you completed them for.   Sharing general positive comments can sometimes be appropriate, but please think about how the fiber producer would feel, and if possible seek their permission to share those comments with others. Confidentiality is so important that the release of confidential information is an offense that can result in revoking your Apprenticeship or Master Certificate.

Working together with other sorters can add to the efficiency of the sorting process. However, poor relationships between sorters can have disastrous results and ultimately drive livestock owners and breeders away from fiber sorting. Avoid public conflict with other sorters and work together in a positive manner to promote fiber sorting. Avoid speaking negatively about other sorters and give positive and constructive suggestions when working in conflict situations. Your fellow sorters are members of your team, treat them appropriately.

BE TIMELY

Being timely refers to not only arriving on time to your job, but also doing your job in a timely manner. In some cases, that means less talking and more working! Don't get caught up in filling space with a lot of words, let your actions speak for you. Do your job by sorting fiber and completing the associated paperwork in an efficient manner.

Often times, it is easier to be timely in live sorting, as it is usually completed during the shearing process. In bag sorting it is important to give the producer an estimated time of completion and stick to it. Holding fiber or untimely sorting when you have committed to a job can result in removal from the Apprenticeship Program or losing your Master Certificate from the SGC program Remember that you are the first step in the production line, and timely sorting and completion of your job (and the associated paperwork) means that the fiber can move on to production and ultimately financial return for the fiber producer that paid your sorting bill.

Being timely also refers to sample submissions to your mentor. It is preferable to send samples each day that you sort. Have an envelope addressed to your mentor and ready for that days samples, then include the proper paperwork and get it to the mail right away. In large sorts, it is helpful for your mentor to receive a few samples over each day as mentors have many students and many samples to check. Once you get your results, get back with the fiber producer in a timely manner, making the corrections and getting their final paperwork to them as soon as possible.

BE ACCURATE

Not only in your assessments, but in your advice. Sorting utilizing the SGC methodology is more than just identifying the grades in a fleece. It is assisting the producer with production decisions, best uses, supplemental information, etc....

Consult your text book. Do research. Know what options are available. Many of your clients are going to be members of fiber cooperatives. If you yourself are not a member, you should still be familiar and up to date with what is available for and required of the member submitting fiber to that cooperative. There are several ways to be more accurate in your sorting. One good practice is to compare your samples against each other. The sample you just said was WL1 should defiantly look smaller than the one you just graded as WL3. The sample you said was WR3 shouldn't look the same as the one you just called WR5. Whenever you are ready to send samples to your mentor a few minutes of self assessment using the above technique will help you move forward faster and understand your own weaknesses. Another essential part of becoming accurate is to collect new samples for your calibration tool. After samples have been handled for a time period they are no longer accurate as contamination or shedding is a by product of use. Keep those corrected "good" samples you run across, using them for future reference.

Finally, a discussion about accuracy wouldn't be complete without mentioning "paperwork"! Properly completing the paperwork in pen, writting neatly, making sure your math is correct is essential. This also includes the required pre education that is to be done with each client. Your sorting is only as good as your recording, and no one enjoys resorting a bag of fiber that was incorrectly labeled or recorded on the inventory sheet incorrectly.

BE COMPLETE - FINISH THE JOB!

The actual act of sorting the fiber really falls in the middle of a well planned and executed sorting job. There are many more things that need to be accomplished to properly complete and finish your job. Although you may not physically be doing many of the jobs in the fiber sorting process, especially in a live sorting situation, you are ultimately the one responsible for each persons job and their performance reflects back on you and your sorting work.

The following list are a few additional things that you need to make sure that they are correctly done during a sorting job:

- Make sure that the bags of sorted fiber are labeled correctly and correspond to the inventory sheet.

- Inventory sheets should be filled out in pen correctly and legibly.

- Go through the Individual Sort Records with the fiber producer, pointing out how to read them and addressing unexpected results.
- Pull samples from each collective bag of fiber sorted according to the protocol and send to your mentor in a timely manner.

- Explain the process to correct bags to the fiber producer if you are unable to correct them yourself. It is helpful to have a handout with examples of how the correction should look on the bag.

- If you have completed your Master Certificate, know that when in doubt you can still send samples.

-

WHEN CORRECTIONS COME BACK FROM YOUR MENTOR

- Make the corrections on the bags or assist the producer in doing this.

- Correct the inventory sheet.

- Additional tasks as required by cooperatives if necessary.

Chapter 2:
DISCIPLINARY ACTIONS

CONSEQUENCES OF NOT DOING YOUR JOB

- ✔ NOT BEING PROFESSIONAL

- ✔ NOT BEING TIMELY

- ✔ NOT FOLLOWING PROTOCOL

- ✔ NOT FINISHING YOUR JOB

NOT BEING PROFESSIONAL

How you conduct your self reflects not only on you but on your fellow sorters and the industry as a whole.   Consider this an ethics policy.

➤ first consequence – verbal warning

➤ second consequence – written warning

➤ final consequence – removal from program.

NOT BEING TIMELY

If you as a sorter, receive fiber for sorting

- and do not complete the sorting in the time arranged,

- do not send off samples for corrections with in 2 days of completion,

- do not make corrections within 2 days of receiving results

- do not upload corrected data within 2 days of receiving results

  - first consequence – verbal warning

  - second consequence – written warning

  - final consequence – removal from program.

NOT FOLLOWING PROTOCOL

Protocol is as follows:

- Pre sort consultation

- Bag or live, you must send the pre-education documents and go over them with the client.

- Fill out the sort records and inventory sheets accurately and completely in pen. (pencil is not allowed)

- As the sorting continues, make sure the bags are being weighed correctly and weights are being recorded accurately as well as labeling of the bags is correct. Even if you are not the one doing this, it is ultimately your responsibility.

- When the sorting is done, go thru the sort records, the inventory sheets, and show them how to play the fiber dating game?. Make sure they have no questions.

- Upload the corrected data from the inventory sheet to the data base.

- If you are an apprentice, you wait to do this until you have received your corrections from your mentor.
- As an apprentice, you must send all copies of paperwork required to your mentor

If a complaint is received for a sorter not doing any of the steps above, you will receive:

  - first consequence – verbal warning

  - second consequence – written warning

  - final consequence – removal from program.

Finishing the job is more than finishing sorting. It means, making sure your client fully understands what fiber they have and what its best uses are.

It means that their fiber is entered into the appropriate data base accurately.

It means returning their fiber to them in a timely manner in the agreed upon condition.

Failing to do any of the above will result in:

➢ first consequence – verbal warning

➢ second consequence – written warning

You will receive an email from SGC giving you an opportunity to present your case, then a decision within 5 days.

➢ final consequence – removal from program.

Your name will be listed as a removed apprentice from the program in all publications.

We hope that these measures will not need to be used. There are many people counting on the integrity of this program. This requires a policy be in place to ensure this integrity is maintained.

Sorting Grading Classing
Creating Standardization Across the USA

I, _____ have read the SGC Policy and Proceedures document and agree to the requirements and conditions listed.

I fully understand that if I break any of the protocols, I will face Disciplinary Action as outlined with the possible removal from the program for repeated offenses.

_____   _____

Candidate Signature   Date

_____   _____

Mentor Signature   Date

The process to become a MASTER SORTER thru SORTING, GRADING, CLASSING (SGC)

Certification/Testing Requirements

Workshop completion:

- Successfully complete the 1 day BASIC and 3 day ADVANCED course
- Pass the written test given at the completion of the workshop with an 80% or better
- Sort fleece while under supervision during the Advanced course

Complete the apprenticeship requirements:

Sort **250 fleeces** using the SGC Methodology

- Sort must include at least 10% Huacaya, 10% suri, 10% wool and 10% other animal fibers of your choice
- Remaining 60% must be an animal fiber discipline of apprentice choice
- At least **125 fleeces must be a "Primary Sort"** –

    A <u>minimum</u> of 20 Live at the Time of Shearing Primary Sort with animal fiber discipline of your choice.

    Sort must include sort for each of 4 fiber types (huacaya, suri, wool, other animal fiber

- 2 years to complete
- Final required – both written and hands on.

PRIMARY SORTER = The sorter that does all the Pre -sort education and Post-sort follow up with the client

SECONDAY SORTER = A helper to the Primary Sorter

LIVE PRIMARY = Sorting is done behind a shearer at the farm at the time of shearing

BAG PRIMARY = All Pre and Post documentation is performed. The sort is completed after shearing either on or off site.

TYPE OF SORT	PPRIMARY	SECONDARY
	Send pre-sorting education documents Identify fiber producers market and processing desire Request the fiber producer to complete a post-sort evaluation Complete all Individual Evaluations and Summary Sheets and discussing the findings with the fiber producer.	All you do is sort or collect fiber, weigh, scribe, etc.
LIVE PRIMARY - Huacaya, Suri, wool or Other Animal Fiber AT TIME OF SHEARING	Minimum of 20 Shorting behind a shearer	
BAG PRIMARY	Not at time of shearing, but all Pre and Post documentation must be preformed	
SECONDARY AT TIME OF SHEARING		Can count towards the total required number of sorts.
BAG SECONDARY		Can count towards the total required number of sorts

The apprentice must also:

- **Uphold the standards of the Policy and Procedure Manual.**
- **Attend at least 1 refresher course**

An apprentice is ready for the final exam when:

- Sorting accuracy is consistently above 80%
- Paperwork is consistently and accurately filed
- Sorting duties are consistently finished in a timely manner
- Completed the required number of Live Sorts, Primary Sorts, and Total Number of fleece.
- Attended at least 1 refresher course.

- Talked with mentor about the final exam, sent practice samples and mentor feels you're ready to test.

FINAL TESTING

Submit a written request to your Mentor for the Final Exam testing along with the fee of $50 (covers postage fees relating to shipping samples to other mentors for review.) A copy of your sort history documenting you have met the number of fleeces requirement (must be signed by the producers) must also accompany your request for the final exam. A packet will be emailed to you with the components for the test.

The final exam consists of two parts. The first is an essay and short answer test. You have 1 week to complete the exam and return to your mentor. A successful candidate should receive 80% or higher to complete this portion of the exam. The second portion of the exam is a skills test. The candidate must send in a total of 40 fiber samples. These samples must include at least 20 huacaya and 20 additional fiber samples that include a combination of wool, suri and at least one other animal fiber type. Note it is your responsibility to procure samples for your exam. Please let your Mentor know if you are having difficulty locating other fiber types to evaluate.

Test samples should include representations from Grades 1 through 6.

The sort record will require an evaluation of grade, You will be asked to give comments relating to the character and condition of the sample as well as it's suitability for textile processing, the best type of processing and make end product recommendations. These samples are reviewed by at least 3 SGC Instructors.

A successful candidate must have 80% or better accuracy on the grade to pass. The assessment test is to be completed and submitted no later than 3 weeks after receiving a passing score on the written portion.

Do not send Mixed Grade samples. Do not send in samples previously evaluated that your mentor has returned to you. **Make sure the bag contains only one grade and that the sample bag is no larger than a sandwich size bag.**

To maintain your MASTER Status you must complete the following:

Uphold the standards set forth in the Policy and Procedure manual.
Attend at least 1 refresher course in your 3 year certification term.

Recertification:

This is done <u>every three years,</u> and is based on fiber sample evaluation. This is a repeat of the same skills test that were given during your initial certification. There is a $50 (covers shipping charges) testing fee which is to be paid at the time of sample submission. All of the above mentioned criteria under "Maintaining your MASTER Status" are to be completed or up to date before the candidate for recertification submits their samples.

How
to
collect
fleece

Client Interview
What you get for
your sorting fee
Well prepared
Alpaca Ranch Shearing Day

PRE-SORTING

Sorting Grading Classing
Creating Standardization Across the USA

Client Interview Planning Survey ✗ Test?

Preparation				
	Yes	No	Not Required	Comments
Have you ever had your fiber sorted before?	☐	☐	☐	
Do you currently do anything with your fiber?	☐	☐	☐	
Do you make your own farm yarns and rovings?	☐	☐	☐	
Have you submitted any fiber to any cooperative? IF yes please list in comments.	☐	☐	☐	
Do you have a retail outlet for your yarns or products?	☐	☐	☐	
Do you currently purchase finished items ie: hats, socks, scarves, gloves from any importer to retail?	☐	☐	☐	
Do you plan to retail alpaca/wool garments in the future?	☐	☐	☐	
Do you knit, crochet, spin, felt or weave?	☐	☐	☐	
Are you willing to invest in value-added to attain a higher profit from your fiber harvest?	☐	☐	☐	
Do you currently do histograms or skin biopsies on your animals?	☐	☐	☐	

WHAT YOU GET FOR FOR YOUR SORTING FEE

(This is the sorting fee per alpaca as it its shorn then sorted.)

1. Yearly harvest of fiber sorted into grades by color and length.

2. Individual sort record for each alpaca with data that includes the weight of each fleece by body area, grades of area, comments on luster/ brightness, density, and uniformity of crimp or lock style, test for tenderness, and sorter comments on the fibers strengths and weaknesses as well as recommended best use.

3. Interactive inventory for the entire clip. The summary provides information on the amount of fiber in each grade, color and length category. This enables the producer to make manufacturing decisions for their clip and allows them to track their farms productivity and average fleece weight / alpaca.

4. Increase in usable fiber. Utilizing the SGC sorting method reduces the amount of fiber that ends up in the garden, burn pile, or trash bin. With good shearing, collection, and sorting, typical waste per alpaca is less than eight ounces per alpaca! Sorted fiber has 10 -15 % less loss in the mill than unsorted fibers. Remember charges for processing may be based on the weight before processing - you pay for the loss that results from processing in increased dollars and reduced product

5. Increase in potential profit. Producers increase profit in several ways:

- More usable fiber per animal.
- Superior products created from sorted fiber command higher prices and repeat customers.
- Sorted fiber has less loss during production.

6. Suggested uses for each grade of fiber. The sorter can assist the producers in recognizing fiber goals, and sort their fiber in a manner that best supports those goals. Appropriate uses for each grade will be discussed, as well as general processing information and resources to assist the fiber producer. The average grade of the fiber herd can be determined, as well as feedback on goals that may have already been set.

7. Assistance with herd management. Because the sorting process is very thorough, external parasites, skin conditions, etc. are identified. Close visual inspection of your fiber also gives clues on times of stress or illness which can in turn help the fiber producer fine tune their herd management.

8. Assistance with breeding decisions. The sort record identified each alpaca's strengths and weaknesses regarding their fiber. The "Alpaca Dating" game, a systemized approach to making individualize breeding decisions is also included and provides the fiber producer a way to improve the strengths and weaknesses of each animal instead of the ribbons they may or may not have won.

Sorting Grading Classing Creating Standardization Across the USA **Copyright © 2016**. All Rights Reserved

17

THE WELL PREPARED ALPACA RANCH FOR SHEARING/SORTING DAY

1. Each person who is assigned a job must stay with that job thru the whole process.
2. You will need to supply the following people.
    a. Fiber collector
    b. A person to record and weigh baskets and bags.
    c. Scribe to write for the sorter (preferably the owner)
    d. Basket runner
        i. This is a minimum.
3. Have on hand clear plastic bags - 33 gal or 55 gal
4. Sorting table (2 if possible - one for blankets and one for necks). Preferred height is 46"
5. An accurate scale that weighs in total ounces or pounds and ounces not pounds and tenths. (I will bring mine!)
6. Large tip Permanent Markers
7. Pens
8. Sufficient Lighting – I will bring my lights as well
9. Extra Clip boards
10. At least 2 large cans of Static Guard.
11. Sandwich bags for histogram samples if you are doing them
12. Gallon bags for spin off samples if you are doing them.
13. Plastic to roll show fleeces in
14. Blank labels to identify rolled fleeces
15. An area out of the weather and wind for the sorter to set up.
16. Minimum of 3 rectangular laundry baskets for fiber collection. These must all be the same size and weight.
17. Collection bins or boxes – 13 of them
18. Trash can

How to properly collect fleece for sorting when a sorter is not available for live sort.

This method can also be used if…
- The weather is inclement on shearing day and fleece needs to dry before being sorted.
- The sorter is behind at live shearing and need to keep fleeces organized until the sorter can catch up.

Supplies needed
1) 55 gal. clear plastic bags (U-line sells them by the box)
    Cut the bottom of the bag, and then cut down one side making a large flat piece of plastic.

    You can also use plastic sheeting that can be obtained at most home improvement stores or brown craft type paper 48" wide available from U Line. Just cut the sheeting in 6' lengths. If planning to ship plastic is more practical

2) Small clear bags for neck fiber
3) 33 gallon clear size bags labeled with Owner ID, alpaca name and color.
4) Black marker

Method
1) **Place the cut plastic 55 gal. bag under the alpaca before shearing begins.** *You can roll the alpaca slightly away from you and easily slip the bag under it. Once the shearer has the blanket on the plastic, slide the plastic out from under the alpaca, towards you. Wrap the top and bottom edges over the fleece so it meets in the middle, making sure the plastic covers the entire fleece. Fold in sides of plastic and gently roll fleece into tight "noodle". The roll can be secured with tape if needed to hold it's shape. Place the roll on the scale and record blanket weight. Place the rolled fleece in properly marked (Owner ID, alpaca name and color) clear 33 gallon size bag.*

2) **Use the small clear bags for neck fiber, making sure to not include any short cuts from lower jaw, and any areas (brisket/chest).**

NOTE: If you are not careful in collecting the neck fiber and inadvertently include all the garbage with it, the usable fiber will become contaminated resulting in higher loss.

3) **Weigh the neck fiber and put the small clear bag in the 33 gallon clear size bag with the rolled up blanket fleece.**

It is very important to have the outside bag labeled with at least alpaca name and color.

Ask your sorter for some sort records to have on hand for shearing day. Fill them out with farm info and alpaca names in the order your alpacas are sheared. As the alpaca is being shorn you need to record the weights of areas of fleece; *(blanket, neck, legs/belly/chest).* Place the record in the bag with the fleece and neck fiber. **DO NOT INCLUDE THE LEG, BELLY, AND CHEST** ("the 3rds", the rug fiber**) IN WITH THE FIBER TO BE SORTED, just record their weight on the individual sort record.**

Proper sheering and fleece collection is the key to maximizing your yearly harvest.

While good shearing will not improve the fleece of your alpaca, poor shearing can ruin it! It is very important that you work with the shearer and the shearer works with you, when gathering the fleece and cleaning up the shearing area.

It is very important to have the basic knowledge of what fiber needs to be collected verses just letting the youngest member of the farm grab your fleeces and throw them into a bag.

It's important to hire a shearer who is will to work with and for you or all your efforts will be wasted and you will be disappointed with the outcome of your harvest.

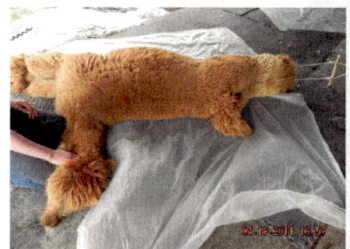
Ready to noodle

Slide fleece away from shearer

Fold one more time

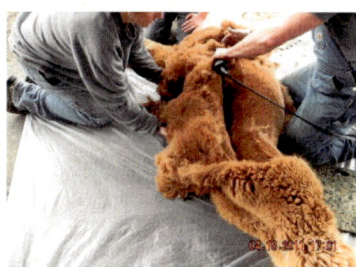
Guide fleece onto plastic

Scrunch fleece to middle to avoid
Contamination of cdgcs on rest of fleece

Roll up fleece

Don't pull just guide

Make sure plastic meets in middle

Tape to keep tight

Sorter Check list   Bag / Live   Primary/ Secondary

Farm Name:_____Contact:_____Date:_____

A checklist of everything a sorter must to do become successful Be prepared! Print this list and check off items as you complete them

Pre appointment:

☐ Pre appointment education docs – bag /live

☐ Pre Sort Questionnaire

☐ Confirmed helpers - live

☐ Confirmed Arrival Time and Directions - live

☐ Attempted to communicate with shearer -live

☐ Ask what they would like to see from their fiber. – bag/live

Sort day

☐ Introduce yourself to shearer – assure that your job is to make the most money possible for the farm as is theirs. - live

☐ Do any last minute training with fiber collector, weight person or scribe. - live

☐ Discuss order of shearing with farm owner and shearer together. - live

☐ Go over sort records and pre education docs with farm. – bag / live

End of Sort Day

☐ Pull fiber samples for mentor to check number of samples sent:_____ - bag/live

☐ Date samples sent to mentor._____ - bag/live

☐ Leave/Send questionnaire with farm with addressed envelope to your mentor bag/live

☐ Thank the shearer for their cooperation – answer any questions they have about what you did. -live

☐ Thank the farm and all the helpers make the most out of this years harvest for this farm. - live

Completion of Sort

☐ Date received results from mentor:_____ - bag/live

☐ Make changes to bags based on mentors corrections – bag/live

☐ Make changes on inventory sheet for client/ keep copy for yourself. – bag/live

☐ Send corrected inventory to farm. – bag/live

☐ Contact Farm for post sort questions.- bag/live

☐ Explain how to use the information on the sort records to help with breeding decisions.

☐ Send a copy of this check list to my mentor bag/live

Apprentice name:_____

☐ Upload sort data for this farm if required by the place they are sending their fiber. Send copy to your mentor – bag/live

☐ Now you are done. – bag/live

Apprentice name:_____

Congratulations! You are taking the first step towards helping develop a North American Natural Fiber Industry and a more profitable farm business! Here are some helpful tips and information to help you make the most of your shearing and sorting day.

What the producer receives with sorting services:

Yearly harvest of fiber sorted into grades by color and length.

Individual Sort Record on each animal with data that includes the weight of each fleece by body area, grade of each area, comments on luster/brightness, and uniformity of crimp, test for tenderness, and sorter comments on the fiber. The individual records are useful in marketing, breeding and general management decisions by the producer.

Inventory sheet for the entire clip. The summary provides information on the amount of fiber in each grade, color, and length category. This enables the producers to make manufacturing decisions for their clip and allows them to track their farms' productivity and average fleece weight per alpaca. Shows your earnings potential for your harvest before your fiber ever leaves your farm.

Increase in usable fiber. Utilizing the SGC method reduces the amount of fiber that ends up in the garden, burn pile, or trash bin. When we first started sorting, most producers were throwing away at least one large bag of fiber per animal. With good shearing, collection, and sorting, typical waste per animal is less than eight ounces! Sorted fiber has 10-35 percent less loss in the mill than unsorted fibers. Remember that charges for processing may be based on the weight before processing – you pay for the loss that results in the processing in dollars and reduced product.

Increase in potential profit. Producers increase profit in several ways:

1. More usable fleece.
2. Superior products created from sorted fiber command higher prices and repeat customers.
3. Sorted fiber has less loss during production. Some mills have commented that the loss from processing is 10-35% less than average.
4. **Suggested uses** for each grade of fiber. The sorter can assist the producer in recognizing fiber goals, then sort fiber in a manner that best supports those goals. Appropriate uses for each grade will be discussed, as well as general processing information and resources to assist the fiber producer. The average grade of the fiber producers' herds can be calculated, giving them feedback on goals they may have already set.
5. **Assistance with herd management.** Because the sorting process is very thorough, external parasites, skin conditions, stress on the alpaca that create fiber breaks, etc., are identified and can be addressed.

At the end of the day, shearing and sorting is completed and a summary of the yearly clip is compiled.

There is no need to skirt the fiber at a later date.
Total weights are recorded by grade, color and method of processing.
Your clip is ready for processing!
Data available to plan for fiber use and address management issues.

Definitions and explanation of terms used in sorting:

WL : Woolen method of processing. Utilizes 1.5 to 3.0 inches in length. Produces lofty yarns with fuzzy appearance. High frequency crimp adds loft to yarn, so fleeces with crimp work best in this application. Woolen processed yarns are best used in sweaters and knitted garments where loft and insulation are desired

WR: Worsted method of processing. Utilizes 3.0 – 6 inches in length. Produces smooth yarn with tighter twist, best used in weaving or lace weight. High amplitude crimp is desirable in this method of processing, and worsted is an excellent method by which to process suri and suri blends

Grade: a group of fibers that have a range of no more than 3 microns.

      Grade 1 is the finest with fibers that are under 20 microns
      Grade 2, fibers are 20-23 microns
      Grade 3, fibers are 23-26 microns
      Grade 4, fibers are 26 – 29 microns
      Grade 5, fibers are 29-32 microns
      Grade 6 – fibers are 32-35microns
      Mixed Grade fibers > over 35 and/or not consistent in lower ranges

FIBER PROCESSING OPTIONS:

Once your fiber is sorted, you can have your harvest processed on your own or you can pool it with others who have sorted fiber.

1. Processing on your own:
   a. Please remember to only blend same grades and same processing method.
   b. Example: WL3 with WL3, but not WR3 with WL3.
   c. Combining with others who have sorted their fiber may help decrease your processing costs by meeting price breaks for larger runs at the mill.
   d. You will have control over the blends and yarns made from your fiber.

2. Processing through a Cooperative:
   a. Lower processing costs because of increased poundage for the run.
   b. Utilizing processors who are experts.
   c. Ability to have finished products made from your fiber.
   d. Product selection is decided by the cooperative including yarn blends.

SORTING

Sorting Grading Classing
Creating Standardization Across the USA

THE WELL PREPARED SORTER

The items you should have with you when you sort can make your experience the best or the worst.

1. Sorting clip board with black/white available whether it is duct tape or paper (bear in mind that paper fades with the sun)

2. Colored paper tags to put in the sorted bags (grade and processing style)

3. Black, large tip markers for writing on the bags.

4. Calculator – in case you have to calculate lbs and tenths into lbs and ounces.

5. Hair ties – makes taking those histogram samples easier and consistent

6. Master copy of the sort record – you should email the ranches ahead of time so they can have the records pre named and in the proper order. But just in case you will have a master to make copies of. On the top write with a yellow highlighter "master copy" (yellow highlighter doesn't copy)

7. Several inventory sheets (have at least 3 summaries / farm)

8. Static guard – this sprayed in the laundry baskets and on your skirting table, even on your hands will help keep the static down.

9. A liquid hand soap that helps limits hang nails.

10. Hand lotion - keeping your hands moist helps with static and keeps the hang nails down.

11. Pens

12. Micron recalibration tool – it is imperative that you recalibrate your eyes at each site.

13. Rubber mats to stand on.

14. A full spectrum light Source: Model #BL42FSWS   Comes in Black can be purchased from SGC.

15. Granola bars, power drinks – keep your energy up.

16. Information about Co-ops. (best to email them the links to websites)

Conversion Table for using Tenths of a Pound

LBS	Total OZ.	LBS	Total OZ
1	16	5	80
1.1	17.6	5.1	81.6
1.2	19.2	5.2	83.2
1.3	20.8	5.3	84.8
1.4	22.4	5.4	86.4
1.5	24	5.5	88
1.6	25.6	5.6	89.6
1.7	27.2	5.7	91.2
1.8	28.8	5.8	92.8
1.9	30.4	5.9	94.4
2	32	6	96
2.1	33.6	6.1	97.6
2.2	35.2	6.2	99.2
2.3	36.8	6.3	100.8
2.4	38.4	6.4	102.4
2.5	40	6.5	104
2.6	41.6	6.6	105.6
2.7	43.2	6.7	107.2
2.8	44.8	6.8	108.8
2.9	46.4	6.9	110.4
3	48	7	112
3.1	49.6	7.1	113.6
3.2	51.2	7.2	115.2
3.3	52.8	7.3	116.8
3.4	54.4	7.4	118.4
3.5	56	7.5	120
3.6	57.6	7.6	121.6
3.7	59.2	7.7	123.2
3.8	60.8	7.8	124.8
3.9	62.4	7.9	126.4
4	64	8	128
4.1	65.6	8.1	129.6
4.2	67.2	8.2	131.2
4.3	68.8	8.3	132.8
4.4	70.4	8.4	134.4
4.5	72	8.5	136
4.6	73.6	8.6	137.6
4.7	75.2	8.7	139.2
4.8	76.8	8.8	140.8
4.9	78.4	8.9	142.4

SORTING RULES 2016

No sorting for fleece not usable due to:

Cotting/Matting/Felting

Tender breaks or dry/brittle fleece

Heavy contamination (VM)

Tightly Twisted locks

Understand the difference between Primaries (P) and Guard Hair (GH) and Secondaries (S)
All GH are Primary fibers but not all Primary fibers are GH.

True GH are stiff, generally straight, don't hold crimp or twist and have a duller color than other
Primaries. GH won't process well into yarns or product, often extending out from the yarn which
may contribute to scratchy/itchy yarn. Primaries will exhibit similar characteristics of the
Secondaries including crimp and twist

Sort for 6 individual grades and a Mixed Grade.

GH - FEW - 3-4.   MANY/NOTICEABLE - 4-6.   Excessive - 7+

Rule 1 - If S and P are within 1 grade of each other grade to S then apply GH Rule

Rule 2 - If S and P are 2 or more grades apart, grade to P then apply GH Rule

Rule 3 - All fiber not meeting these requirements will be sorted to mixed grade and likely be
hairy requiring dehairing. (Yield may be low)

GH Rules –

- GH should be evaluated based on quantity within draw or draft.

- If draft/draw has FEW TO NONE, grade to Rule 1 or 2. May or may not dehair

- If draft/draw has MANY/NOTICEABLE grade to Rule 1 or 2 if being dehaired.
  If not dehairing or unsure at time of sort, drawn sample should be graded to
  highest grade present (S,P,GH)

- If draft/draw has EXCESSIVE, drawn sample should be graded to Highest grade
  present (S, P, GH) and advise owner the need to dehair this batch. If it is KNOWN
  that fiber will be dehaired, grade to P knowing there will likely be decreased yield.

- **SURI** fiber does not dehair effectively. All **SURI** fiber should be graded to the above
  rules applying the non dehairing GH rules.

Inventory Sheet.

DATE		Last name			Farm Name			Sorter Name			No of alpacas	
Farm email :												

01 - WHITE 02- BEIGE 03 - LT FAWN 04 -M. FAWN 05- D FAWN 06 - LT BROWN 07 - M BROWN 08 -D BROWN

09 -LT GREY	10-M.GREY	11.D GREY	12. LT R GREY	13. M R GREY	14. D R GREY		15. BAY BLACK	16. TRUE BLACK	17 NATURAL BLACK			
Bag #	Huacaya or Suri	Color	Grade	OZ	TOTAL BY GRADE	Bag #	Huacaya or Suri	Color	Grade	oz	Bar Code	
1						49						
2						50						
3						51						
4						52						
5						53						
6						54						
7						55						
8						56						
9						57						
10						58						
11						59						
12						60						
13						61						
14						62						
15						63						
16						64						
17						65						
18						66						
19						67						
20						68						
21						69						
22						70						
23						71						
24						72						
25						73						
26						74						
27						75						
28						76						
29						77						
30						78						
31						79						
32						80						
33						81						
34						82						
35						83						
36						84						
37						85						
38						86						
39						87						
40						88						
41						89						
42						90						
43						91						
44						92						
45						93						
46						94						
47						95						
48						96						

Soot Recochs

Form 1:

ANIMAL NAME	SHEAR DATE:	LAST NAME: FARM NAME: EMAIL	SORT DATE	SORTER NAME	SORTER#

BLANKET WEIGHT — NECK WEIGHT — LOWER LEG, BELLY, CHEST — 3.5 — TOTAL USABLE FIBER PRODUCED

BLANKET GRADE:
S-
P-

NECK GRADE:
S-
P-

TENDER: Y or N ___ Cria fleece ___ Primaries > ½ Y / N ___ Primaries > ½ Y / N
only on edging

LUSTER 1-10	UNIFORMITY OF CRIMP/LOCK STYLE 1-10	CPI	AMPLITUDE L M H	LENGTH	TEXTILE COLOR

COMMENTS: ___ Too Contaminated ___ Lots of second cuts ___ Too long or short for processing
___ uniform in grade ___ clean well prepared Thanks!

Form 2:

ANIMAL NAME	SHEAR DATE:	LAST NAME: FARM NAME: EMAIL	SORT DATE	SORTER NAME	SORTER#

BLANKET WEIGHT — NECK WEIGHT — LOWER LEG, BELLY, CHEST — TOTAL USABLE FIBER PRODUCED

BLANKET GRADE:
S-
P-

NECK GRADE:
S-
P-

TENDER: Y or N ___ Cria fleece ___ Primaries > ½ Y / N ___ Primaries > ½ Y / N
only on edging

LUSTER 1-10	UNIFORMITY OF CRIMP/LOCK STYLE 1-10	CPI	AMPLITUDE L M H	LENGTH	TEXTILE COLOR

COMMENTS: ___ Too Contaminated ___ Lots of second cuts ___ Too long or short for processing
___ uniform in grade ___ clean well prepared Thanks!

NOTES

Shear order form

Inventory

Sort Record

Ranch signature

Well prepared sorter

Sorter Check list

Pre appointment

Sort Day

End of Sort Day

Completion of Sort

What you get for
your Sorting
Day

POST-SORTING

FORMS THAT GO TO THE FARM

Sorting Grading Classing

Creating Standardization Across the USA

Interpreting Your Sort Records   *Post Soct*
                                     & Pre soct

Weights: gives an indication of the useable fiber your animal produces and can be compared year-to-year. Blanket weight is the prime body area including shoulder and hip areas. Neck fiber is very usable. Often times it can be even more uniform than the blanket. Leg, Belly and Chest refers to areas that have strong primaries or guard hair necessary to protect the alpaca from the elements but is too hairy to be used for products or yarn for things that will touch the skin.

Brightness: How does the fleece react when held under the light. Brightness refers to ability to shimmer or reflect the light.

Uniformity of Crimp/Lock: determined by comparing the 6 samples pulled from different areas of the fleece and is an indication of how similar they are. Are they uniform not only in crimp or lock style from cut end to tip, but are they uniform in staple length.

Crimps per Inch and Amplitude of Crimp: self-explanatory. For suri, lock structure may be documented here.

Density: very difficult to interpret just from a fleece but indicators can be observed by how well the fleece holds together, thickness of the staples, or volume of fleece on the table.

Color: this is textile color and not necessarily the same as the ARI color chart that is used to determined show or registration color. For example, white fleece with some black primaries would be grey since the black would stand out in an otherwise all white yarn.

Tender: if the lock can be broken by pulling it along its long axis, it will break during carding and spinning and create bumps/slubs in the yarn. Tender fleece in adults could mean a health issue is present. Cria fleeces that have never been shorn often have tender tips.

Primaries > ½": this indicates a hairy fleece and will need to be dehaired before yarn creation to decrease the fibers that stick out from the yarn. These fibers can make the yarn feel coarser and prickly.

Secondaries & Primaries

Grade 1   up to 20 microns
Grade 2   20-23 microns
Grade 3   23-26 microns
Grade 4   26-29 microns
Grade 5   29-31 microns
Grade 6   31- 35 microns
Mixed Grade>35 microns or a mix of several micron sizes in the fibers

The number(s) in the final grades reflects the relationship of the grades of the secondaries and primaries. If the primaries are only one grade or less stronger (larger) than the secondaries and they are scarce, the final grade will be that of the secondaries. If they are close in size but numerous, it will be the grade of the primaries.

If the primaries are stronger than the secondaries (or extend more than ½ inch past the secondaries) then the fleece is hairy and needs to be dehaired during processing.

WL: woolen length for processing. 1 ½ inches to 3 inches

WR: worsted length for processing. 3 inches to 6 inches

Examples:

    WR4   fiber length 3 - 6 inches; 26-29 microns

    HWL2   fiber length 1 ½ - 3 inches; 20-23 microns; and
                 Hairy so the primaries are coarse and/or long

All of this information gives you another way to evaluate your alpacas and can help you with breeding decisions to improve the quality of fleece in your herd. While fineness should be one of the factors, of at least equal importance is uniformity and lack of hairiness. Those two last qualities will increase the value of the fleece because it can be directly processed into yarn without the waste and extra expense of dehairing.

Hopefully the sorting process and discussion of the uses of the different grades leads to an understanding that fleece that is coarse by alpaca standards still can be profitable. Thank you for giving me the opportunity to sort your fleece.

Post sort questionnaire

1. Was the experience what you thought it would be?

Explain.

2. Has your perspective about fiber changed in anyway?

Explain.

3. What things would you change about the sorting experience?

Explain.

4. Would you have your fiber sorted again?

Explain.

5. Your overall feelings or additional comments?

Please return this questionnaire to:
(put your mentors contact info here)

Fiber Match Maker

Using your sort record for help in making breeding decisions;

1. Separate into 2 piles, males and females.

   A. Using a highlighter of 1 color on the males, highlight all positive traits for each male.

   B. Using a different color highlighter, highlight each males negative traits.

2. Do the same thing with the female pile except switch colors.

   This will instantly show which traits of the male will complement the negative traits of the female.

Front of sort record

Name: Male A	Farm: Serenity Farms	Date: today
Blanket grade:S 2, P 4 <3 WL3 primaries > ½ inch Y N 68 oz	Neck Grade: S 2P 4 <3HWL3 primaries > ½ inch Y/N 28oz	Mid leg grade
Lower leg Belly and chest weight. 54 oz	Total weight 9 lbs 6 oz	Sorter Name Suzie Q Sorter # 821
Comments: Very uniform in grade and crimp style. Appears to exhibit density		
Luster: 7	Uniformity of crimp style 8	

Example: Male A.

Back of sort record

POSITIVE:	NEGATIVE
Uniform grade from the blanket into the neck. (S and Ps are the same) No long primaries in blanket Good weight in legs, belly and chest Sorter noted good density	lacking in Luster Long primaries in neck

Front of sort record

Alpaca name: Female A	Farm ; O boy alpacas	Date: today
Blanket grade: S 3 P 4>4 WL 4 primaries >1/2 inch Y/N 31 oz	Neck grades 5 P 5 <3: WL5 primaries > ½ inch Y/N 20 oz	Midleg grade oz
Lower leg, belly and chest 33 oz	Total weight: 5 lbs 4 oz	Sorter Name: Suzie Q Sorter # 821
Comments: Lacking in density		
Luster 8	Uniformity of crimp style 6	

Back of sort record

POSITIVE	NEGATIVE
Has good lustre	Lacking in Density Not Uniform grade from the blanket into the neck. Long primaries in blanket and neck

FINAL CRITERIA;

- Double check to make sure they do not have the same negative fiber traits.
- Check conformation on both male and female. Be sure you don't breed two that are similar in weaknesses.

Example 2:

Front of sort record

Name: Male B	Farm: Serenity Farms	Date: today
Blanket grade:S 1 P 2<3 HWL2 primaries > ½ inch Y/N 69 oz	Neck Grade:S 3 P 5<3 HWL4 primaries > ½ inch Y/N 33oz	Mid leg grade
Lower leg Belly and chest weight. 60 oz	Total weight: 10 lbs 2 oz	Sorter Name Suzie Q Sorter # 821
Comments: Very uniform in grade and crimp style.		
Luster: 8	Uniformity of crimp style: 8	

POSTIVE	NEGATIVE
Uniform crimp style Luster	Longer primary length in blanket and neck Higher grade in neck Blanket and Neck grade as Hairy due to extending primaries

Female B.

Front of sort record

Nname: Female B	Farm : Serenity Farms	Date: today
Blanket grade:S 3 P 5<3 WL 4 primaries >1/2 inch Y/N 31 oz	Neck grade:S 4 P 5<3 WL4 primaries > ½ inch Y/N 20 oz	Mid leg grade oz
Lower leg, belly and chest 33 oz	Total weight: 5 lbs 4 oz	Sorter Name: Suzie Q Sorter # 821
Comments: Lacking in density, needs uniform crimp style		
Luster 8		Uniformity of crimp style 6

Back of sort record

POSITIVE	NEGATIVE
Uniform in grade from neck to blanket Luster No long primaries in blanket or neck	Lacking in density Lacking in uniformity of crimp style Higher grade in neck and blanket

Although at first glance, Male B appears pretty spectacular, the blanket fiber is pretty fine and he scores really high in brightness and uniformity of crimp style. On the negative side, his neck is 2 grades higher than the blanket and his primary fibers extend beyond his secondaries. This indicates that he lacks uniformity which is the number one thing we should be breeding for.   This would not be a good breeding decision.

Focus on improving 2 traits / breeding on the females. Take your breeding program up in steps for more consistent results.

Outside breedings: When considering outside breedings, ask to see that stud's sort record. If they do not have one, offer to have that blanket and neck sorted so you will have that information.

Apprentice Sample Results			Apprentice Name		
Farm Last Name					
Bag #	Apprentice Results	Apprentice Color	Actual Results	Comments		
1						
2						
3						
4						
5						
6						
7						
8						
9						
10						
11						
12						
13						
14						

Apprentice Name: _____

Class Date: _____

Date	Fiber Producer Name	Primary Live Sort Huacaya	Primary Bag Sort Huacaya	Seconday Sort Huacaya	Primary Live Sort Suri	Primary Bag Sort Suri	Seconday Sort Suri
	Apprentice Class						
Total							

Mentor: _____

Primary Sort Wool / Other	Ranch Signature
	42

NOTES

How to Documents

Sorting Grading Classing
Creating Standardization Across the USA

How to use your calibration samples

Each time you start sorting pull out these samples and look at them to calibrate your eyes to sample grades. Spend a little time comparing how they look drawn across your board at your preferred sorting distance under your light. Look at the diameter of the secondary on your finger tip and make mental reference to its appearance. Do this for all grades and you will soon get the visual dialed in.

These samples were put together to the grade of the secondary, not the final grade based on how the secondary and primary relate in the sample. Ignore the primary in the calibration sample.

When you start sorting and need clarification refer to the sample to determine the grade of the secondary. Then determine to the grade of the primary.

For example: If you think the secondary is a grade 2 and compare to the grade 2 calibration sample and it is the same, then continue. If it looks bigger refer to the grade 3, and so on.

If you think the primary is a grade 4, then compare it to your grade 4 calibration samples.

Once the grade of the S and P are identified, refer to the Sorting Rules to apply final grade.

How to use your calibration samples

Each time you start sorting pull out these samples and look at them to calibrate your eyes to sample grades. Spend a little time comparing how they look drawn across your board at your preferred sorting distance under your light. Look at the diameter of the secondary on your finger tip and make mental reference to its appearance. Do this for all grades and you will soon get the visual dialed in.

These samples were put together to the grade of the secondary, not the final grade based on how the secondary and primary relate in the sample. Ignore the primary in the calibration sample.

When you start sorting and need clarification refer to the sample to determine the grade of the secondary. Then determine to the grade of the primary.

For example: If you think the secondary is a grade 2 and compare to the grade 2 calibration sample and it is the same, then continue. If it looks bigger refer to the grade 3, and so on.

If you think the primary is a grade 4, then compare it to your grade 4 calibration samples.

Once the grade of the S and P are identified, refer to the Sorting Rules to apply final grad

Sending Samples to Your Mentor

- Sort your fiber into collective bins. (WL1-WL6 and WR1–WR6)
- Samples must be pulled for all sorted grades (do not send mixed grade samples) on **every** sort.
- At the end of the sorting session (not the end of the farm) complete the following

Take a sample from each collective bag you sort – please have at least a handful of fleece, **taking fleece from several parts** of the bag so as to give a good representation of the overall bag **(do not send samples from individual alpacas).**
The sample bag (a sandwich size bag) should be about half full of fiber.
Put the fiber in the sample bag and label with inventory number as well as this info:
Bag #, Grade, Color, Farm owners last name, your name and date
Example:

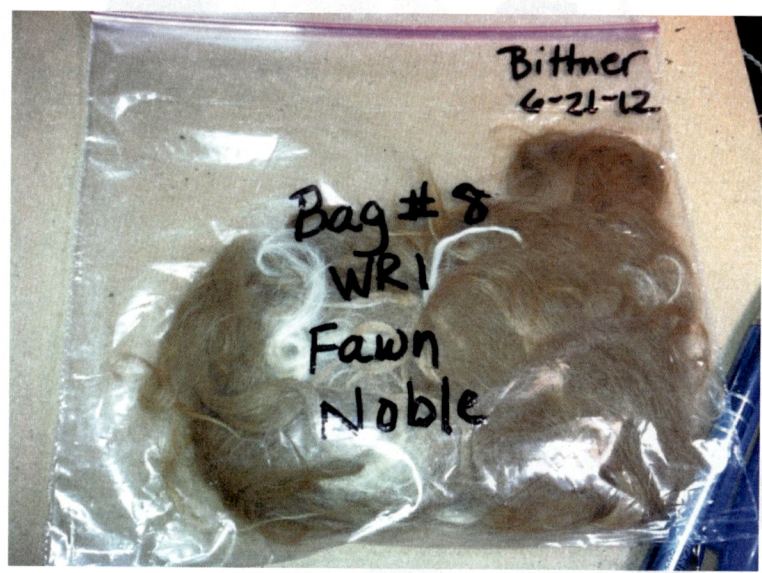

The bag # from the Sort Inventory **is the number** on the **sorted** bag and also on a sandwich size **sample** bag.

It is helpful and good preparation for your test, to also include your S and P grade as well as anything that you used to determine grade - example: S2 P4 <3 in a pull – on the WL3 bag and if it has extending primaries over ½ inch. This can only be done if you review your samples before you send them in - it is recommended that you do that if time is permitting.

Fill out the excel document **Apprentice Blank Results Form**
This form summarizes the samples that you will be mailing to your mentor. This information is the same info that will be on your inventory sheet. Your mentor will fill in the results and email back to you

Apprentice sample results				apprentice name			date			
farm last name										
bag #	apprentice results	apprentice color	actual results	comments						
1										
2										
3										
4										
5										
6										
7										
8										
9										
10										
11										
12										
13										
14										

When you email this form to your mentor let them know how the sort went. Was the sort done in at your farm or was it at another farm, how was the lighting, set up, etc. Was anything different from the last time you sorted?

Mail your samples, with a copy of the inventory sheet so your mentor can see the weights of your bags

When you are completed with a sort, also send a copy of the sorter check list that you have been using during the sort. This lets your mentor know you are done and can assist you in completing the follow up and data entry for the finished sort

IMPORTANT POINTS:

- SEND SAMPLES FREQUENTLY or if sorting on weekends, that Monday so can have results back by the time you sort the following weekend
- SEND ENOUGH FIBER SO YOUR MENTOR CAN GIVE YOU AN ACCURATE ASSESSMENT
- SEND THE PROPER PAPERWORK WITH YOUR SAMPLES
- EMAIL THE RESULTS REPORT TO YOUR MENTOR SO YOU CAN GET YOUR RESULTS QUICKER
- MAKE THE CORRECTIONS AND REVIEW YOUR MISTAKES AS SOON AS YOU GET YOUR RESULTS BACK – DON'T WAIT!!!
- ENTER THE SORT DATA RIGHT AWAY WHEN SORT IS COMPLETE – DON'T WAIT!!

After receiving results from your mentor make your corrections as follows:

1. Go back to the producer and make changes on the bags or resort the bags that were incorrect if directed to do so.

2. Change info on bag and mark out previous grade with an X.

3. Make change to inventory sheet as needed, if you have additional bags from resorting, add them to the inventory sheet at the end of the already listed bags.

4. Make sure that you have numbered the bags according to the inventory sheet.

5. Provide the producer with a correct inventory sheet, keep a copy for yourself to be able to enter data to the database from.

NOW YOU ARE READY TO ENTER THE SORT DATA IN THE DATA BASE

- Enter the corrected sort information into the database within a day or two of making the corrections. DO NOT WAIT ON THIS – GET IT DONE!
- Please type in the bag numbers in the note section on the individual fiber entries.
- Remember that the fiber cannot be submitted to the RCF without being Entered into the data base.
- Finally - Notify your mentor that you have uploaded the data to the database for the fiber sort.

Let your client know the fiber is ready to go to the RCF.

Revised 2/11/2016

Putting it all Together

1. Organize your Pre-Sorting Paper Work
   Make a file on your computer so can print or email easily
   Make a file with up to date printed copies to have at finger tips

What you get for your $15
Sample Shearing order
The well prepared sorter for shearing day
Proper Fleece Collection doc

Client Survey
Mailing information to fiber producer
The well prepared alpaca Ranch for Shearing Day

Great time to discuss with client what their goals are for their fiber

2. Prepare for Sort
   Print off sort records with farm information, your name, and dates
   If doing live sort or planning before shearing date gives producer form to print
   Have them fill out for each alpaca sorting in advance
   Print off inventory sheet with farm information and your name
   - Make sure have enough new bags and all other supplies needed for the sort
   - **Sorting rules cheat sheets**

   While sorting, pull samples and update the inventory sheet every time you complete a color

3. Post- Sort
   Apprentice need to: Refer to Sending **Samples to Your Mentor Document**
   Double check samples pulled from bags
   Properly mark them with
   Bag # that corresponds with inventory sheet
   Grade and color and farm name
   Your name
   Date

Fill out **Blank Results Form (Excel Doc.) to be emailed to Mentor prior to mailing samples**
Include comments of how the sort went in the email along with the Blank Results Form
Bag numbers should all match inventory sheet and sample bags and email to mentor
Mail all sample to mentor along with the following documents:
Inventory Sheet
***Include the check list with the last batch of samples sent. This will alert your mentor that the sort is completed and they can then help you finalize the sort

Promptly after receiving results
Correct the inventory sheet
Correct bags with proper grade, and color

Enter Sort into Data Base for NFP Members

Documents that help communicate results to producers

How to use sort summary for breeding decisions – Fiber Match Maker
Can also refer back to **Mailing information to fiber producer document** for grade and usage clarifications
Post sort Survey for them to send to mentor and have them sign **sort history** for recording your sort numbers

If you take the time to get organized and familiarize yourself with this document flow you should have no problem conforming to the standardization process to become a certified sorter.

Start with just 3-5 fleeces and work thru entire flow.   Practice you pre-sort and post-sort presentation for these fleeces with another sorter, friend, spouse, or even you favorite pet to gain confidence. Your clients will love you and want you back if can tell them what they have, what they can do with it, and how they can profit from it.

ATTRIBUTES	DEFINITION	POSITIVE EFFECT ON PROCESSING	NEGATIVE EFFECT ON PROCESSING	HOW WE ASSESS IT DURING SORTING
LUSTER	The ability of a fiber to reflect light. Typically a result of the size of the scale and how adhered it is to the fiber shaft – the bigger the scale and the closer to the fiber shaft the more light reflection	Produces a shiny effect on the yarns. Knitted has less reflection than woven. Also improves the handle as the scales are large and flat.	Can be harder to spin due to larger scales (slippery fiber as the scales don't grab each other as readily)	Subjective measure – compares animals on that farm to each other. Good 7,8,9 Fair 4,5,6 Poor, 1,2,3
UNIFORMITY OF CRIMP/LOCK STYLE	2 Assessments: Uniformity within the 6 samples and also from cut to tip of the staples. Do the 6 initial samples have the same/different crimp or lock style? Are they the same from cut end to tip?	Crimp can assist in ease of spinning by holding on to a neighboring fiber. Open lock style is much easier to process	Tight pencil locks that encompass at least half the lock cannot be processed and affect the processing ability of other fibers in the batch.	Subjective measure – compares animals on that farm to each other. Good 7,8,9 Fair 4,5,6 Poor, 1,2,3
CRIMPS PER INCH	Expressed as CPI – refers to how many hills OR valleys in an inch.	Higher frequency crimp adds more loft and insulation so is best processed woolen. Lower frequency assists drape and tighter twist so is best processed worsted		Choose 2 -3 staples to count either hills or valleys – not both. Can assist producer in identifying health issues – "hiccup" Give a range: 4-5
AMPLITUDE	The height of the wave or crimp	Lower amplitude results in higher frequency in more air pockets or insulation. Higher amplitude results in a greater ability to compress the fiber thus resulting more drape and tighter twist		Subjective Measure expressed as low, medium or high a combination of two - Low-Med

DENSITY	Density refers to the closeness or compactness of the fibers in a fleece. The more fibers per square inch, the denser the fleece	No affect on processing – density only affects the producer		No exact measurement to date. Consider: -Cohesiveness of the fleece -Size/Weight of fleece compared to body size -Hand-full test -# of S to P in a lock -Ability to see the skin when fleece is parted -Lock Compression
TEXTILE COLOR	Based on the color of individual fibers with the fleece. See textbook for a complete description.	When fibers are condensed in processing the colors of the individual fibers can amplify or become more visible.	Occasional "off-colored" are not desirable in a solid color run such as black or white.	Not based on ARI color chart. Recorded on the sort record to assist the producer in breeding and shearing order
FIRE RETARDANT	The lack of ability to ignite and burn easily			We do not assess during sorting. This attribute would be discussed in post sort summary with producer
NATURAL REGAIN	The ability of the fiber to absorb moisture before the wearer notices a change in temperature		There is a reason towels are made out of cotton	
STRENGTH	Length of fiber and the amount of twist in a yarn also influences strength	Stronger fibers will process more easily and not break.	A weak fiber creates weak yarns, pilling, and / or slubs	7 lbs of pressure is the key number to determine a weak fiber Pencil size locks are tested
INSULATIVE	How much fiber is required to achieve a certain insulative factor			
WRINKLE RECOVERY	The ability of a fiber to resist wrinkling			
WEIGHT	The weight of fiber is measured as their weight in relation to water expressed by their specific gravity	Lighter weight fibers will make lighter weight garments	Heavier weight fibers will make heavier weight garments	
MEMORY	The ability of a fiber to return to its natural state after stretching			

NOTES

Made in the USA
San Bernardino, CA
16 May 2016